Christmas Jazz, Rags & Blues

8 arrangements of favorite carols for late intermediate to early advanced pianists

MARTHA MIER

Jazz is an important and distinctive American contribution to 20th-century music. *Christmas Jazz, Rags and Blues, Book 5,* contains 8 arrangements that reflect the various styles of the jazz idiom. Students will love the challenge of playing some of their favorite Christmas songs in the jazz style.

Jazz is fun to play! Students will be inspired and motivated by the syncopated rhythms and the colorful, rich harmonies of jazz—a style which has captured the imagination of performer and listener alike!

Martha Mier

Alfred Music
P.O. Box 10003
Van Nuys, CA 91410-0003
alfred.com

ISBN-10: 0-7390-7354-0
ISBN-13: 978-0-7390-7354-4

God Rest Ye Merry, Gentlemen

Traditional English Melody
Arr. by Martha Mier

WE WISH YOU A MERRY CHRISTMAS

Traditional
Arr. by Martha Mier

WE WISH YOU A MERRY CHRISTMAS

Traditional
Arr. by Martha Mier

Toyland

Victor Herbert
Arr. by Martha Mier

Away in a Manger

John R. Murray
Arr. by Martha Mier

Deck the Halls

Welsh Carol
Arr. by Martha Mier

Go Tell It on the Mountain

Spiritual
Arr. by Martha Mier

18

O COME, ALL YE FAITHFUL

John F. Wade
Arr. by Martha Mier

20

Hark! the Herald Angels Sing

Felix Mendelssohn
Arr. by Martha Mier